BALLAGH / Robert

An Leabharlann Chathartha, Corcaigh

Leabharlann Chathair Chorcaí

3 0007 00082 968 8

REFERENCE DEPARTMENT

CLASS R 941·83 A/NO N85925

THIS BOOK is provided for use in the Reference Room
only, and must not be taken away. It is earnestly
requested that readers use the books with care, and
do not soil them, or cut, tear or turn down leaves, or
write or make any marks on them or otherwise damage
them. The habit of wetting finger or thumb to turn
leaves should especially be avoided. The use of the
Reference Room is subject to the Rules and Bye-Laws;
and any injury to books, or any improper conduct,
will be dealt with as therein provided.

COLEMANS   C210

D1612813

DUBLIN

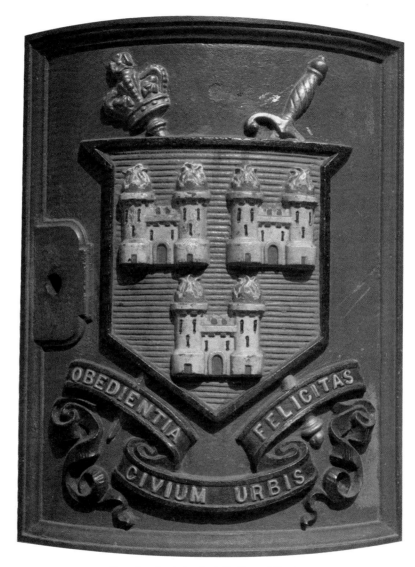

Base door, lamp standard, Parliament Street

Robert Ballagh

DUBLIN

Introduction by
Ciaran Carty

Ward River Press, Dublin 1981

Foreword and captions, copyright © Robert Ballagh 1981
Introduction copyright © Ciaran Carty 1981
Photographs copyright © Robert Ballagh 1981

Designed by Joseph Kelly

Colour separations and plates, Litho Studios Limited

Printed in Ireland by Cahill Printers Limited

Ward River Press
Knocksedan House
Forrest Great
Swords
Co. Dublin

ISBN   0 907085 15 6.

N 85925

Contents

*To my wife, Betty, and children, Rachel and Bruce,
who share with me the pleasure and pain of living in
Dublin city*

"For myself, I always write about Dublin, because if I can get to the heart of Dublin I can get to the heart of all the cities of the world. In the particular is contained the universal."

James Joyce.

FOREWORD

It was just over ten years ago when I bought my camera. It seems strange now that it was simply chance that caused me to buy the particular camera that I still use today. At the time I needed some slides of my paintings and, not possessing a camera myself, I persuaded a camera shop near my studio to lend me one. It was a second-hand Rolleicord made in 1954. After the shots were taken I returned the camera and waited a few days for the results to become available. I was so impressed that I practically ran all the way back to the camera shop, determined to make a purchase, fearful that the camera might have been sold already. I was in luck and paid all of twenty-five pounds for the best investment I ever made.

For several years I simply used the camera to take slides of my paintings, and it was in fact a shift in the development of my painting that initially caused me to expand my photographic experience. In about 1972, I began a series of paintings which incorporated the human figure. I remember that I used to collect cuttings from newspapers and magazines for reference material, but of course this was most unsatisfactory as I could spend ages scouring through magazines looking for one precise reference that I needed for a painting. It was a while before the obvious solution occurred to me: to take the photograph myself. This had the dual benefit of not only providing an exact reference but also peopling my canvasses with my family and friends! I suppose this use of the camera is similar to the sketch pad of the traditional artist, with the advantage, however, that unlike the selective approach of the artist the camera records everything without distinction.

For many years the camera was simply another tool that I employed for my painting, and it was not until 1979 that I decided to use it for another purpose. That winter I was invited by the State Department to visit the United States, as part of a visual arts programme. Not being the kind of person who keeps an interesting and informative diary, I decided instead to bring my camera and record the experience. To my delight and amazement some attempts resulted in photographs that not only communicated something of the experience but could also stand on their own merit. It was on seeing these photographs that my publisher, Philip MacDermott, set in motion thoughts that finally resulted in this book. We had previously discussed the possibility of making a book about Dublin, perhaps using drawings or paintings. However, the personal approach evident in the American photos convinced Philip of the possibility of a new photographic book on Dublin.

He did not indicate any particular approach but left everything up to me. I decided, rather than adopting any preconceived notions, that I would simply bring my camera everywhere with me for twelve months, the duration of the project. This practice has resulted quite naturally in a totally subjective view of Dublin. For this I make no apologies. In fact not only have I photographed the ordinary places that I encounter every day, but I have assiduously avoided photographing the celebrated views that are already well represented in existing books.

It was some time before I noticed any general approach becoming apparent. But eventually it struck me that I was unconsciously excluding people from the photographs that I was taking. This seemed doubly odd in that my approach to painting is exactly the opposite; I am in essence a painter of the human figure. Besides, nowadays the streets of Dublin are continually packed with both cars and people. It was something I noticed while re-reading Walter Benjamin's essay "The Work of Art in the Age of Mechanical Reproduction" that enabled me to make sense of this apparent anomaly. In discussing the early Paris cityscapes of Eugene Atget, Benjamin remarked, "it has quite justly been said that he photographed them like scenes of crime". This view of the street as being quite literally a stage-set for the enactment of human drama is very interesting, because it inevitably leads one to the conclusion that if the *dramatis personae*, namely the citizens, are introduced then attention shifts quite naturally away from the set which, in my case, is Dublin.

So in photographic terms, to get close to what D. H. Lawrence called "a spirit of place", it is perhaps necessary to exclude the very people who help make the city a living organism. Nevertheless, living as I do in the inner city, an area rich in the sort of "characters" for which Dublin is rightly famous, I must admit that I was tempted to include some colourful people in this book. I felt that this subject matter would be overly sentimental and far too anecdotal. But it was a personal experience that finally convinced me. Some time ago I saw two very young travellers buying a magazine which contained a fairly harrowing article with photographs about travellers' children who were involved in glue-sniffing. When they saw the photographs they exclaimed, "Oh, there's Mary, look at Billy!" I asked them had they ever sniffed glue. They replied "Oh no, sir." I remember thinking at the time how impressed they were with all the publicity, and wondering just how soon it would be before they too copied the habits of their momentarily famous friends.

Another aspect of contemporary Dublin that gets scant attention, I'm afraid, in this book is the steady erosion of the fabric of the city. This absence should not be seen as an indication of personal lack of interest and commitment.

Rather, I feel that the matter could be dealt with more effectively elsewhere. An example of the speed of the current erosion is the fact that several of the places photographed for this book during 1980 have since been totally changed or demolished. This was not the case in the Dublin of the 1950s where I grew up—a city almost unchanged from the Dublin so accurately recorded by James Joyce half a century earlier.

To Joyce, the city of Dublin and its people were an obsession. He went to great lengths to record them with total accuracy. He frequently wrote from Paris to his aunt asking for exact information concerning places that he was about to describe while writing *Ulysses*. In exile he prided himself on his ability to "name the shops from Amiens Street to the Pillar, first one side, then the other". Yet just as he transformed this Dublin into the world in microcosm, so too he charged the insignificant with significance.

This ability to see something special in the simplest of things has also been my goal in the preparation of this book.

Robert Ballagh.

August 1981

INTRODUCTION

Robert Ballagh is a painter who happens to take photographs.

There are artists who hesitate to admit using a camera as if to do so might in some way take away from their art. To resort to mechanical aids is seen by purists as a form of cheating. For Ballagh painting and photography are simply two different ways of creating images: there is no valid reason why one should be regarded as fine art and the other as something else.

"An artist stands or falls by what hangs on the wall," he once told me. "If the image on the wall is interesting or significant—or whatever one demands from a work of art—it doesn't matter whether he used X-ray film or charcoal on toilet paper to create it. It's the image that matters and what that image communicates to the observer."

Photography has influenced painting and sculpture since the first primitive prints appeared early in the last century. Indeed one suspects that the *camera obscura* was not unknown to Vermeer and some of the Dutch masters long before that.

Delacroix welcomed the new medium as "a remedy against mistakes". Corot experimented with glassprints to study the movement of wind in trees. Degas's horses are derived from Muybridge's celebrated sequences of action photographs illustrating locomotion. Monet, Cezanne, Gauguin, Toulouse Lautrec, Picasso, Warhol, Rauschenberg and Henry Moore all embraced photography as a medium for expanding their vision. The way we see—and the way the painter sees—is pervaded by photographic influences. Snapshots, newspaper pictures, advertising layouts, movies, television and video merge into an all-enveloping environment from which—like passive smoking—no one is immune.

Robert Ballagh in particular was steeped in mechanically produced images as a child. They were the real source of his cultural education, the only college of art he ever attended. He'd never miss a matinee at the Ritz cinema in Ballsbridge and his parents would take him to double bills as a regular treat. He lived for the *Eagle* comic every week ("you always got a beautiful airbrush drawing of an aeroplane or a ship spread across the centre pages"). The only paintings he experienced were colour reproductions in books his father borrowed from the nearby RDS library.

Second-hand music was another source: the whole rock 'n' roll phenomenon of the 1950s on treasured 78s. While still at school he strummed skiffle at tennis hops. He quit architecture at Bolton Street to play bass guitar professionally with the Chessmen—and soon had a record in the Top Ten.

He always had a facility for drawing and painting. His teacher John Coyle at Blackrock College had told him he could become a painter if he wanted to. A meeting with Michael Farrell at Toners pub in 1967 prompted him to give it a try.

By then Ballagh was about to marry Betty Carabini and the hectic glamour of being a pop star—by twenty he was earning what seemed big money and driving a flashy car—had begun to pall. "One night I realized that in the course of a whole gig I hadn't played a single tune I liked. My taste was progressive rock but all the fans wanted to hear was country-and-western."

Farrell, fresh back from New York and spreading the brash gospel of hard-edge acrylic brightness, let him mix paints and help out on two huge murals he was completing for the Bank of Ireland. "The experience was short-lived but it inculcated in me a sense of being an artist," Ballagh recalls.

Ballagh's impact was to be as immediate as an unknown rock singer zooming straight to the top of the charts. By applying the abstract techniques of acrylic work he had learned from Farrell to simple figurative ideas, he created a distinctive pop language that was both an honest and natural response to his own experience and completely new in Irish art.

His very first works—painted metal constructions of a female torso and a pinball machine—were promptly accepted by the Living Art. The Arts Council bought an acrylic painting of a blade, to the outrage of some critics. He was commissioned to paint screens for the UCD cafeteria and murals for the new Fitzwilton offices. A diamond painting from the 1968 Living Art—his only purely abstract work—was bought for the Bank of Ireland collection.

Each of these works was an exercise in problem-solving, a matter of learning as he went along. But his attitudes outside art—his socialist involvement—would not permit him simply to indulge in art for art's sake.

By 1969 he had developed the vocabulary to say more than purely formal things. His paintings became statements, with a series of split images of civil rights marches (he had himself taken part in several), burning monks in Vietnam, refugees and firing squads, which gave stunningly direct expression to the social consciousness of the decade. He won the Carrolls Prize at the Living Art and was chosen to represent Ireland at the Paris Biennale.

Ballagh came to art without any of the usual indoctrinated notions, seeing it as a job like any other job ("I'm not the kind to think it's my role to be a genius starving in a garret"). He has been less held back by the romantic inhibitions about integrity that limit more traditionally trained artists.

He used anything and everything that works

to produce an image, realizing that in the end it's the image that matters and not how it has been produced. The source of his 1969 paintings in particular was photographs culled from newspapers and magazines. But he soon began using a camera—as other painters use a sketch pad—because it was too much of a chore finding ready-made shots of the images he needed.

Unable to get proper portrait likenesses of Gordon Lambert or David Hendriks, he screen-printed photographs of their faces instead. He openly plagiarized some of the great masters—Goya's "Third of May", Delacroix's "Liberty at the Barricades" and David's "Rape of the Sabines"—to create starkly apt comments on the North's internecine conflict. For his audacity he won the Alice Berger Hammerschlag Award.

Ballagh has none of the customary hang-ups about compromising his independence by accepting commissions. "I love the idea of art being used, and if it's commissioned it will be used." Portraits of Hugh Leonard, Bernadette Greevy, James Plunkett, Brendan Smith and Charles Haughey became a way to develop a language that led to more autobiographical work of his own.

He parodied conventional taste with paintings of leopard skins and iced caramels, introducing low-art kitsch to the high-art setting of the David Hendriks Gallery. He then parodied the avant garde establishment with a virtuoso series of people looking at work by Rothko, Pollock, Vasarely, Gnoli, Wesselman, Stella, Lichtenstein and many of the other brand names of contemporary art.

"The whole thing was for me an examination of Modernism. By the time I finished I'd lost faith in a lot of its shibboleths. I had an intuitive feeling that I was no longer a Modernist painter. I had been hidebound by a philosophy that stood in the way of developing according to my own nature."

Yet ironically it was with this farewell to Modernism that he acquired an international reputation as a Modernist painter, exhibiting at the Aktionsgalerie in Bern, the Galerie Isy Brachot in Brussels, the Galerie Liliane Francois in Paris and the Nicholas Treadwell in London.

All his work since has been an attempt "to reconnect" with the great tradition of geometric perspective handed down since the Renaissance but rejected as redundant by the Modernist cult of the "Briefly New" (which dictates that each new "ism" automatically invalidates all that has gone before).

Beginning with images inspired by Sterne's *Tristam Shandy* (direct literary quotation: the ultimate sin against contemporary formalism), he engaged in visual dialogue with traditional masters like Vermeer ("The Conversation") and Velazquez ("Winter in Ronda"): the fundamentals of Western art became for him a medium with which to express contemporary and increasingly personal concerns (as shown, in particular, by "Inside Number 3").

By reverting to such a commonly accepted visual language—people have being seeing in this way for 500 years—his art has become accessible through reproduction to a much wider audience. "If you're involved in visual communication, the logic is to communicate to the greatest number of people," he likes to say.

That is what draws him to photography too: its power to disseminate images beyond the élite world of the unique art object and the gallery-dealer-critic system.

But there is perhaps a deeper connection. The images in this book, with their haunting sense of the mark of time on streets and buildings, reflect a growing preoccupation with place (also evident in his painting: he used landscape elements for the first time in a recent portrait).

Ballagh's urge to record, with the documentary fidelity of the camera, and his feeling of empathy with the Dublin he has lived in all his life, stem from a concern with identity and the whole nature of Irishness.

The radical economic and social changes brought about by the Lemass-Whitaker Programme of Economic Development and by Donogh O'Malley's opening up of education to the masses (to say nothing of the challenging impact of television) have abruptly transformed Ireland from a predominantly agricultural, Church-ridden, backward-looking people into an industrialized, urban, European consumer society with an affluent and questioning middle class.

With the emergence of indigenous publishing and local patronage, it is now becoming possible to root art in an Irish experience free of the traditional romantic myths and conformity to international requirements. Within this context the work of Robert Ballagh, now mid-term in his career, takes on a timely significance.

It would be ironic indeed if a painter originally castigated for the "unIrishness" of his pop imagery should now in the 1980s come to embody what Irishness in art really is, not something imposed through false sentiment, like a thatched cottage in a landscape or a Celtic motif in hard-edge abstraction, but a sensibility arising out of the social reality of the artist.

It is no longer necessary to agonize about the things that seemed so insurmountable in the 1950s: Gaelic Ireland, the Church, censorship and the whole naive de Valera belief that the twentieth century was not for the Irish people because the Irish people were not in the main interested in the things of the flesh but rather those of the spirit.

"It's almost as if all those veils have been lifted and there it is: this is Ireland, deal with it!

"The most important thing an artist can be is to be honest with himself. If he does that he'll rise above all these other questions.

"But he cannot avoid responding to the environment in which he lives, and if this environment is Ireland or Dublin or wherever, the work will reflect this if it is done honestly."

Even the most abstract art bears the mark of a time and a place: it is a social product. The artist in Ireland, perhaps for the first time since the foundation of the State, is now free, to deal honestly with the reality in which he finds himself. His view, as much as that of any politician or economist, is needed to articulate what Ireland is about.

That is the function of Robert Ballagh.

Ciaran Carty

Ciaran Carty is art editor and deputy editor of the *Sunday Independent*. His forthcoming biographical study of Robert Ballagh is to be published in 1982 by Ward River Press.

"riverrun, past Eve and Adam's. . ."

Adam and Eve's is the Franciscan Church on Merchant's Quay built in 1834, its architect being James Bolger. Like many places in Dublin its popular name is not in fact its official one, Church of the Immaculate Conception, but derives in this case from the fact that the entrance to it was through a public house which bore that sign. In the photograph the church is viewed through a narrow lane which leads from High Street down to the back of Adam and Eve's and thence on to the River Liffey.

Schoolhouse Lane West, off High Street

The River Liffey viewed from Grattan Bridge, popularly known as Capel Street Bridge

Adam and Eve's faces across the river to the splendid drum and dome of the Four Courts and to "the poor stunted houses like a band of tramps huddled together along the river banks, their old coats covered with dust and soot, stupefied by the panorama of sunset and waiting for the first chill of night to bid them arise, shake themselves and begone" (*Dubliners*).

The River Liffey between Islandbridge and Chapelizod (I)

A favourite walk of mine is along the south bank of the river, and during the fishing season, come hail or shine, keen anglers are crowded along the banks striving to land the enviable prize of a Liffey salmon. The path is also used by rowing trainers who belt along on bicycles, shouting instructions to their teams on the water.

The River Liffey between Islandbridge and Chapelizod (II)

In the background stands the Wellington Testimonial, the "*duc de Fer's* overgrown milestone", a massive 205-foot structure standing in the Phoenix Park. Robert Smirke's imposing design was chosen by competition and paid for by public subscription.

The River Liffey below Butt Bridge

To many Dubliners the Liffey not only links the city but also divides it. Growing up on the south side I was made aware from an early age that things were not quite the same across the river. It seemed to me that most south-siders viewed the north city as some sort of waste land, where nothing of consequence ever occured. Even the great buildings on the north quays like the Four Courts and the Custom House seem to agree and turn their backs on the north city. In fact the cinemas and ice-cream parlours of O'Connell Street and the occasional funeral in Glasnevin were often the extent of most southern incursions into the north city. For my part, when I married and came to live on the north side I discovered a portion of the city which was rich in detail and history.

Avenue leading to Memorial Park, Islandbridge

Before moving on towards the sea, I would like to pause in order to point out a favourite haunt of mine on the banks of the Liffey, the Memorial Park at Islandbridge.

The Memorial Cross, Memorial Park, Islandbridge

This is one of the few places featured in the book that caused me to make a special excursion. I woke up early one Sunday morning and saw outside an unusually bright fog. I immediately dressed, grabbed my camera and drove up to Islandbridge. Whilst lacking detail I feel the results convey something of the atmosphere of the place.

CORK CITY LIBRARY

Trees below the Memorial Park on the Liffey banks

original design by Sir Edwin Lutyens. The whole of the work was carried out under the direction of Mr. T. J. Byrne, principal architect to the Board of Works in the Irish Free State. The Memorial was officially opened, after a number of postponements, on Armistice Day 1940.

On to the Sea

Drinking fountain, Ringsend

It is only the inhabitants that know and indeed use all the place-names that go to make up a city. Dublin has a rich crop of names which must appear quite strange to the outsider. Arbour Hill, Ballsbridge, Chapelizod, Dolphin's Barn, Marino, Oxmantown, Portobello, Ringsend, Stoneybatter and Windy Arbour are just a few random samples.

Lamp standard, Ringsend

Ringsend still retains the quality of being a village in a city, and the locals jealously guard their independence. During my childhood Ringsend was the destination of all excursions that ranged south along the Dodder River, and it also formed the gateway to many further delights.

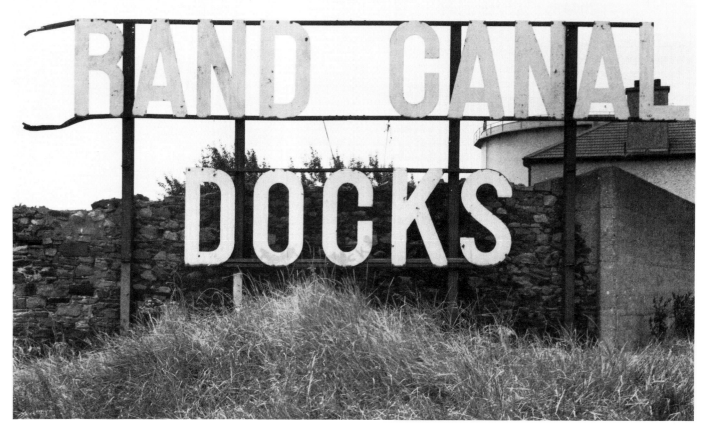

Ringsend

The trip down to the Poolbeg lighthouse along the South Wall was and still is one of my favorite walks. The Grand Canal Dock which is reached by descending some stone steps at Ringsend Bridge and crossing a series of gushing lock gates remains an amenity of enormous but unfortunately neglected potential. At the north end of the basin stands the Dublin Gas Company, today a relatively tranquil place, but in its coal-burning days it was a cauldron of noise, fire, steam and smell, which in turn earned it the nickname "Dante's Inferno". It was believed that the sulphurous fumes which emanated from the gas works could cure many a childhood ailment: "Whooping cough they say it cures" (*Ulysses*).

The South Wall

Poolbeg lighthouse

As early as 1800 Captain William Bligh, R.N., better known for later exploits on the *Bounty*, surveyed Dublin Bay and proposed the erection of the north and south retaining walls to improve the harbour. At the time the plan was not accepted; however, the overall design that was finally executed by the Ballast Board closely resembles Bligh's original concept.

The South Wall

"His feet marched in sudden proud rhythm over the sand furrows, along by the boulders of the south wall. He stared at them proudly, piled stone mammoth skulls. Gold light on sea, on sand, on boulders" (*Ulysses*).

The Half Moon Swimming Club

During the Napoleonic War a half-moon shape was cut from the South Wall. This implacement became known as the half-moon battery. A shelter for soldiers who manned the gun was also erected. In 1898 the Poolbeg bathers were established and when they took over the old shelter in 1910 they changed their name to the Half-Moon Bathers Club. The block house beside the swimming club was erected during the Second World War and contained an alarm system which warned of approaching ships.

The Bull Wall

Shelter, Bull Wall (I)

The Bull Wall forms the northern part of the Ballast Board's plan for improving the harbour. It was completed in 1825. The Bull Island, which stretches northwards from the wall, contains an immense sandy beach, two golf courses and a wild-life sanctuary of considerable importance, all within a few miles of the city centre. I first discovered the Bull during my days as a student when, to escape the bustle of city life, I used to withdraw to places like Dollymount Strand in order to contemplate life and its consequences. Perhaps this is one of the reasons why the writings of James Joyce strike such a personal chord.

Shelter, Bull Wall (II)

It was here on Dollymount Strand in 1898 that James Joyce heard the call of his real vocation. As Stephen in *A Portrait* he describes how he was moved with a feeling of profane joy on seeing a young girl with her skirts pinned up, gazing out to sea: "Her image had passed into his soul for ever and no word had broken the holy silence of his ecstasy. Her eyes had called him and his soul had leaped at the call. To live, to err, to fall, to triumph, to recreate life out of life! A wild angel had appeared to him, the angel of mortal youth and beauty, an envoy from the fair courts of life, to throw open before him in an instant of ecstasy the gates of all the ways of error and glory. On and on and on and on!"

Clontarf marina

Across the water lies the South Wall and the new Poolbeg electricity generating station. In fact the two chimneys are now the most prominent landmarks in Dublin and can be seen plainly from almost every neighbourhood.

New beach beside Poolbeg generating station

When the new power station was being built on the South Wall, I was terribly afraid that the massive construction involved would be detrimental to the local environment. However, happily, the South Wall can now boast of two new beaches instead. This photograph shows "the lace fringe of the tide", with Sandymount Strand and the Dublin and Wicklow Mountains in the far distance.

Costelloe's Landing, the South Wall

Dublin is uniquely served by its geographical situation, for in a matter of minutes it is possible to be either at the seaside or to be walking in the mountains which surround the city.

Resting Places

Seat, the King's Inns, Broadstone

Any city of consequence should provide worthy resting places, both final and otherwise, for its citizens. Dubliners are well accommodated in this regard. Local people always refer to the King's Inns as "the Temple". This is interesting as I'm convinced that the name comes from the local landlords, the Temple family, and not from the similarly named institution over in London.

Park gate, the King's Inns, Broadstone

There are certain qualities that only time can give to a city. Places like the King's Inns provide ready evidence not only of Dublin's age but also record the constant passage of her citizens over the years.

The King's Inns

In *Dubliners* James Joyce described "the decrepit old men who drowsed on the benches" and "the children who ran screaming along the gravel paths" of the King's Inns. This clearly shows that, in spite of the passage of time, some things simply don't change. The background features not only my house but also St. Mary's Chapel of Ease, known to most Dubliners as the Black Church. Austin Clarke, who grew up in the locality, called his autobiography *Twice Around the Black Church*. This refers to the local custom which maintains that if one runs around the church at midnight, the devil will appear.

Bandstand, Herbert Park, Ballsbridge

This park was laid out for the Dublin Exhibition of 1907 on land originally belonging to the Earl of Pembroke whose family name was Herbert. My earliest memories must be of Herbert Park for I can vaguely recall being wheeled along in my pram and being shown the ducks.

Herbert Park, Ballsbridge

Every childhood pastime was tested in Herbert Park. We sailed ships in the pond, we flew model airplanes near the bowling green and close by indulged our greatest but nonetheless illegal passion—speedway racing. We charged around in circles on our push-bikes attempting to emulate our heroes the Shelbourne Tigers, from nearby Shelbourne Stadium, until inevitably we were chased off by an irate gardener.

Book room, Memorial Park, Islandbridge

Lutyens built a granite pavilion at the ends of each pergola to contain books in which the names of the dead were written. Today these pavilions are vandalised and the books are gone.

Pergola, Memorial Park, Islandbridge

Unfortunately the park has been neglected in recent years. Perhaps the present authorities are somewhat embarrassed by a memorial to the forgotten Irishmen who fell in the First World War. Anyhow, the only people who now use the park continually are teenagers holding drinking parties and travellers grazing their horses.

Shelter, Botanic Gardens, Glasnevin

The Royal Dublin Society opened its Botanic Garden at Glasnevin in 1795. It was taken over by the State in 1878. I really like the enormous glassed conservatory with the sweaty smell of giant palms and an almost overpowering heat, "with sleeping sickness in the air". However, it was this little bye-corner in the gardens, not much frequented, that caught my eye.

St Stephen's Green (I)

In the seventeenth century St Stephen's Green was part of a green belt "wholie kept for the use of the citizens and others, to walk & take the open aire". Its design was "chiefly for the reputation, advantage, ornament and pleasure of the cittie" (Maurice Craig, *Dublin 1660–1860*).

St Stephen's Green (II)

". . . the trees in Stephen's Green were fragrant of rain and the rainsodden earth gave forth its mortal odour, a faint incense rising upwards through the mould from many hearts" (*A Portrait*).

Mount Jerome (I)

"How many. All these here once walked around Dublin. Faithful departed. As you are now so once were we" (*Ulysses*).

Mount Jerome (II)

Cemeteries are places usually avoided by the living on the conjecture that as one inevitably ends up in a grave, why tempt fate by calling early? In spite of this, I have a great attraction to the old part of Mount Jerome.

Mount Jerome (III)

There is a quiet dignity surrounding Mount Jerome Cemetery. Nothing about it appears ostentatious or overpowering, unlike Glasnevin Cemetry where massive momuments and tombs ensure that those civil and ecclesiastical authorities who dominated the Irish so completely in life will do the same in death.

Mount Jerome (IV)

"All honeycombed the ground must be: oblong cells. And very neat he keeps it too, trim grass and edgings. His garden Major Gamble calls Mount Jerome . . . . I daresay the soil would be quite fat with corpse manure, bones, flesh, nails, charnelhouses. Dreadful. Turning green and pink, decomposing. Rot quick in damp earth. The lean old ones tougher. Then a kind of a tallow kind of a cheesy. Then begin to get black, treacle oozing out of them. Then dried up. Deathmoths" (*Ulysses*).

Mount Jerome (V)

". . . Saddened angels, crosses, broken pillars, family vaults, stone hopes praying with upcast eyes, old Ireland's hearts and hands" (*Ulysses*).

"Lift Up Thine Eyes"

South City Market, George's Street

The indiscriminate despoliation of the city at street level, caused by the proliferation of gaudy new shops all competing for trade, is inclined to blind us to the fact that above eye-level little has changed over the years. Those who look up can often find excellent examples of the architecture of a bygone age. The Victorian eccentricities of the South City Market are thankfully still intact.

Sunlight Chambers, Parliament Street

In 1928 Lever Bros began to manufacture soap in Ireland. Before this they operated on a sales and distribution basis, importing products from Port Sunlight in England. Their headquarters were here in Parliament Street.

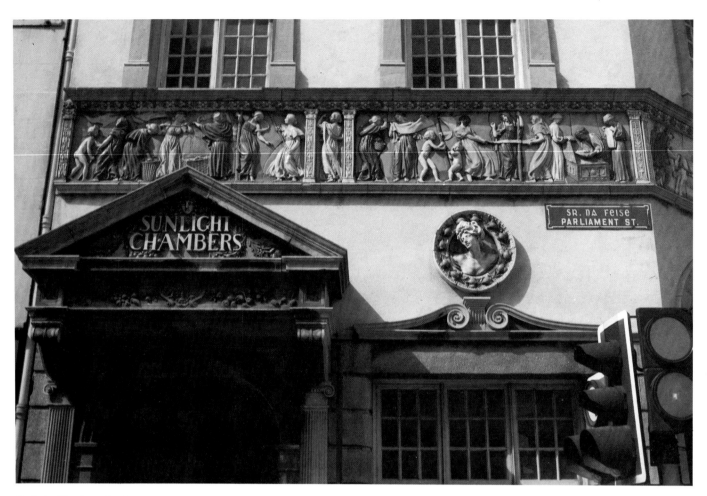

Sunlight Chambers, detail

The elegant neo-Florentine design of Sunlight Chambers is decorated with beautifully executed ceramic friezes depicting a very mundane subject indeed, namely, "washing through the ages".

Sick and Indigent Roomkeepers Society, Palace Street

Today the term "roomkeeper" appears somewhat ambiguous. In fact it refers to those poor who, because of their circumstances, were forced to find accommodation in single rented rooms. The society was founded in 1790 for the relief of all denominations in the city of Dublin, which earns it the reputation of being Dublin's oldest charity. The building in Palace Street has been under a compulsory purchase order for ten years, and this order has seen the gradual erosion of all the surrounding properties. Nevertheless, the society still clings tenaciously to their present premises.

The Corporation Fruit Market

Every morning I am lucky to be able to walk through the fruit market on the way to my studio. The smell and appearance of the fresh fruit and vegetables are enough to brighten the start of even the darkest of days. This photograph was taken on a Sunday, the only day that the place is not bustling with activity.

Onions

I had originally planned to photograph one of the wholesalers' displays inside the market, but I felt that the results would inevitably resemble the commonplace illustrations of travel magazines. Instead I decided to use the lovely terracotta designs featuring fruit, vegetables and fish which are dotted around the building.

Carrots

"Thither the extremely large wains bring foison of the fields, flaskets of cauliflower, floats of spinach, pineapple chunks, Rangoon beans, strikes of tomatoes, drums of figs, drills of Swedes, spherical potatoes and tallies of iridescent kale, York and Savoy, and trays of onions, pearls of the earth, and punnets of mushrooms and custard marrows and fat vetches and bere and rape

Pears

and red green yellow brown russet sweet big bitter ripe pomellated apples and chips of strawberries and sieves of gooseberries, pulpy and pelurious, and strawberries fit for princes and raspberries from their canes'' (*Ulysses*).

Duty-free warehouse, North Anne Street

In recent times the manufacture of whiskey has been moved out of Dublin, but these warehouses remain, storing the whiskey in barrels until it reaches maturity, "not a drop sold until it's 12 years old".

Private Places

Homeville, Rathmines

As human beings we require not only companionship but also, at times, solitude. A large city, paradoxically, is one of the few places where an individual can enjoy real privacy.

Cook Street

Who can guess what dramas unfold behind a facade such as this? The private lives of the occupants always remain the business of nobody but themselves, but though the lace curtains carefully maintain an interior privacy they can always be "dragged aside" to quickly re-establish a link with the world outside: "an old woman peeping. Nose whiteflattened against the pane" (*Ulysses*).

Tattoo Artist, Capel Street

This strange and very personal art is practised by Johnny Eagle, here at 82 Capel Street, every day excepting Wednesday and Saturday on an unending stream of eager customers.

Nolan's, Mespil Road

In the past the local shop was a focal point in the community and, as such, provided a service that was often social as well as commercial. Unfortunately, many have failed to survive in the battle with the brash and less personal supermarket traders, and once the struggle has been lost, the shops become sadly vacant—dusty windows, empty shelves.

High Street (I)

For a time abandoned premises simply remain vacant, a condition not without hope since with effort they can be brought back to life. However, when they become boarded up little chance remains for resuscitation.

High Street (II)

These two facades were painted for the papal visit of 1979. All the vacant and boarded-up shops looked so shabby that it was decided to brighten them up. Ironically it was to no purpose as the Pope's tour failed to keep to schedule and passed by in the dark!

Doorway, Dominick Street

This quite extraordinary example of the plasterer's art, by sheer coincidence, happens to be almost opposite Dominican Boys Home at number twenty, whose interiors contain some of the finest pieces of plaster decoration in Dublin, the work of Robert West, master builder and stuccodore.

7 Eccles Street

Behind this door and to the back was once the bedroom of Molly Bloom. Her private nocturnal meditations in this room fill the final pages of *Ulysses*. This house, celebrated in literature, has fallen, the victim—along with much of the neighbourhood—of planner's blight and civic indifference.

St. Michan's National School, Cuckoo Lane

I'm sure there are many who have enduring private memories of the time spent attending this old school. However, my own associations with the place are anything but scholastic; at election time I come here to place my vote in the ballot box.

House, Church Street

This individual flight of fancy is to be found at the corner of Church Street and Stirrup Lane, part of a small attractive housing development between Church Street and Beresford Street which was one of the first to be undertaken by the Dublin Corporation.

Post Office, High Street

High Street was once the main thoroughfare of the medieval city, but has become much less important today. The roadway has been widened into a dual carriageway so that people in cars are encouraged to speed past; consequently the buildings that line the street receive scant attention. This post office has closed down since the photograph was taken.

M. Carroll, Clanbrassil Street

Until quite recently you could buy almost anything here, for "Carrolls of the bridge" was one of those wonderful hardware shops that carried an extraordinary variety of stock. Brushes hung from the ceiling, buckets, paint tins, boxes were stacked in profusion on the shelves—now, alas, no more.

Vicar Street

Window, Sandycove

Fishamble Street

In Dublin the craftsmanship of the eighteenth- and nineteenth-century granite paving is of the highest European standard. In recent years, however, the corporation has seen fit to replace the granite paving with the much more mundane concrete slab. Derry O'Connell expresses the hope "that the self-cleaning, beautiful quality of the remaining granite may be re-appreciated by the Paving Department and retained" (*The Antique Pavement*).

St Francis Xavier's Girls Club, Gardiner Place

I love the faintly threatening note to this declaration. It seems to suggest that during the novena only those who have paid will be prayed for.

Midland Hotel, Broadstone

The Broadstone Station was the terminus for railway travellers from the west. When it closed in 1931 it left behind "a melancholy quarter of high and dry hotels" (Maurice Craig, *Dublin 1660–1860)*. The Midland was one of the last to close its doors. Happily, after much refurbishing, it has reopened.

St Mary's Place

The Black Church casts its shadow over this row of neat cottages. It was designed by John Semple and dates from 1830. The interior features an incredible parabolic vault which replaces both walls and ceiling.

Window, Temple Cottages, Broadstone

These "blotchy brown brick houses" are Dublin Artisans Dwellings. During the nineteenth century many reforms were introduced to improve the living conditions of the peasantry. However, in the cities the situation of the working classes was largely ignored; Dublin had some of the worst slums in Europe, with thousands of families crowded into single-room tenements. To counteract this, the Dublin Artisans Dwelling Co. was established.

Epiphanies

Lamp standard, Henrietta Street

Stephen Dedalus tells Cranley in *Stephen Hero*, as they stand before the Ballast Office, that its clock "is capable of an epiphany" or "a sudden spiritual manifestation", though "only an item in the catalogue of Dublin's street furniture".

Light bracket, Broadstone

"Dublin possesses a remarkable collection of little-noticed street objects, of 18th, 19th and early 20th century aesthetic interest, all still in common use" (Derry O'Connell, *The Antique Pavement*).

Reads, Parliament Street

Perhaps the oldest family business in Dublin. First established in 1670 on Blind Quay, Reads later moved to Crane Lane in 1750. When Parliament Street was developed the shop was literally turned around. The original trade was in swords and halberds, which finally gave way to cutlery. But for quite some time Reads produced much-prized surgical instruments. The shop still contains three original Chippendale cabinets.

The Irish Yeast Co., College Street

Molyneux Yard, Thomas Street

Winch, Grand Canal Dock

This winch is one of several which still operates the three locks between the Liffey and the Grand Canal Dock. The lock gates were built in 1796, and this date along with the names of each particular lock, Westmoreland, Buckingham and Camden, are handsomely carved in the granite side walls.

Bovril Building, Ringsend

I remember as a child gazing in wonder at the Bovril electric sign which was high up on a building opposite Trinity College. The name was constructed from coloured bulbs and then surrounded by an amazing fan-shaped array of multi-coloured lights

Kodak Building, Rathmines

There is still some early modern architecture left in Dublin, but the disappearance of the Imco Building on the Merrion Road is a worrying sign of possible future destruction. There is, after all, no "Art Moderne" Preservation Society.

Kildare Street Club (I)

In Ireland the nineteenth century produced a rich crop of fine craftsmen who, within the constrictions of the total design, were often given great leeway in the execution of their work. A fine example of this are the humorous carvings on the base of the windows of the former Kildare Street Club.

Kildare Street Club (II)

Recently an over-robust cleaning job has unfortunately damaged many of the carvings. The superb interior of the building, designed by Deane & Woodward, has also been gutted and destroyed to accommodate modern offices.

Betting Office, The Red Cow, Clondalkin

While driving home from Cork one evening I saw this extraordinary prospect. Perhaps the many hours of childhood spent watching movies has conditioned the way that I see things; certainly this particular photograph has all the appearance of a scene from the American West.

Points of Departure

Bus Station, Store Street

Most of the weary travellers waiting for buses at this station are probably unaware of the many delights provided by architect Michael Scott. Busárus was one of the first major modern buildings to be designed in Europe after the Second World War.

Crane, Poolbeg lighthouse

The Poolbeg lighthouse marks the entrance to Dublin harbour. All vessels arriving or departing must pass this point.

Colonnade, Broadstone Station

If asked to pick out a favourite building in Dublin, without hesitation I would nominate the Broadstone Station, designed by John Skipton Mulvany. Maurice Craig suggests that it is "the last building in Dublin to partake of the sublime. It stands on rising ground, and the traveller who sees it for the first time, so unexpected in its massive amplitude, feels a little as he might if he were to stumble unawares upon the monstrous silences of Karnak or Luxor" *(Dublin 1660–1860)*.

Broadstone Station (I)

Maurice Craig maintains that "in purely architectural terms it is hard to praise it too highly. As one mounts the slope the great pylon-like block of the main building arrests and holds the eye; then to the right the seemingly interminable colonnade carries the imagination towards the flat bogland of the Central Plain—to the countless sleepy stations, Kilcock, Moyvalley, Killucan, Streamstown, Ballinasloe, Ballyhaunis or Claremorris, to the cattle-pastures of Westmeath and the wide solitudes of Longford and Roscommon". He suggests that "much of the poetry of travel perished when the Broadstone was abandoned in 1931" *(Dublin 1660–1860)*.

Broadstone

The station now lies marooned on the hill opposite the King's Inns, its link with the city having been removed many years ago. The place where this viaduct, which also carried a spur of the Royal Canal (remembered locally as the aqueduct), entered the station forecourt is in the centre of this photograph.

Mooring post, Grand Canal Dock

It is still possible to enter this basin from the Liffey, then motor westwards and eventually link up with the Shannon north of Banagher in Co. Offaly.

St. Audoen's Gate

Built around the year 1240, this is the only surviving city gate, and dates from the period when Dublin was a walled town.

White Rock, Vico Road, Dalkey, Co. Dublin

The river which began the book has now run its full course into the waters of Dublin Bay and in turn becomes "a commodius vicus of recirculation". I have fond memories of the Vico for I used to bicycle the eight or nine miles to White Rock almost every day during the summer holidays from school. The Vico Road runs south from Dalkey around Killiney Bay and finally out of Co. Dublin towards Bray, Co. Wicklow.

Acknowledgements

I would firstly like to thank all those anonymous fellow Dubliners who freely volunteered both advice and assistance during the preparation of this book. I hope the final result reflects in some way their commitment to and enthusiasm for Dublin city.

For permission to quote from the works of James Joyce I am indebted to the literary representatives of the Joyce Estate, the Society of Authors, and to the following publishers: Faber & Faber (quotations from *Finnegans Wake*), The Bodley Head (quotations from *Ulysses*), Jonathen Cape (quotations from *Portrait of the Artist* and *Dubliners*). I am grateful to Maurice Craig for permission to quote from *Dublin 1660-1860* and to Derry O'Donnell for permission to quote from *The Antique Pavement*.

I would especially like to thank those friends who generously surrendered their time when I asked for help with the difficult task of preparing the text. Any accuracy in the architectural information is due to Dr Edward McParland of T.C.D. and to Nicholas Sheaff of the National Trust Archive. The advice offered by Kieran Hickey proved invaluable in the structuring of the text. Noel Carroll of Dublin Corporation obtained much necessary information. I would also like to thank all at Ward River Press (Philip MacDermott, Cormac Ó Cuilleanáin, Adrienne Fleming and Margaret Daly) for their consistent help and continuing enthusiasm during the project, Joseph Kelly for his assistance in design & layout, as well as acknowledging David Davison's much-appreciated photographic help and advice. Finally, I must thank my wife Betty for her support, advice and unending patience, which must have been sorely tried, during the writing of this book.

Robert Ballagh photographed on O'Connell Bridge

All the photographs reproduced in the book were taken during 1980–1981. The camera used was a twin lens reflex Rolleicord, without additional lenses or filters. I always photographed using available light, frequently a difficult task, for as Simon Dedalus remarked the skies of Dublin are "as uncertain as a child's bottom". *(Ulysses)*

INDEX   Each entry lists the name, the map reference where applicable (see pages 124-125), and the pages on which the name is mentioned.

Index compiled by Helen Litton

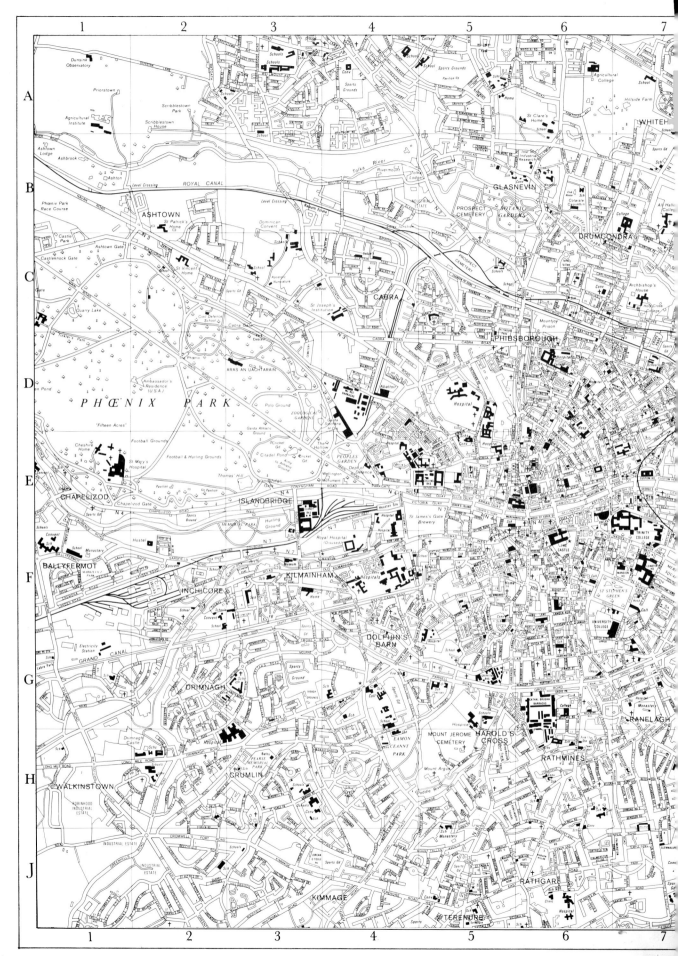

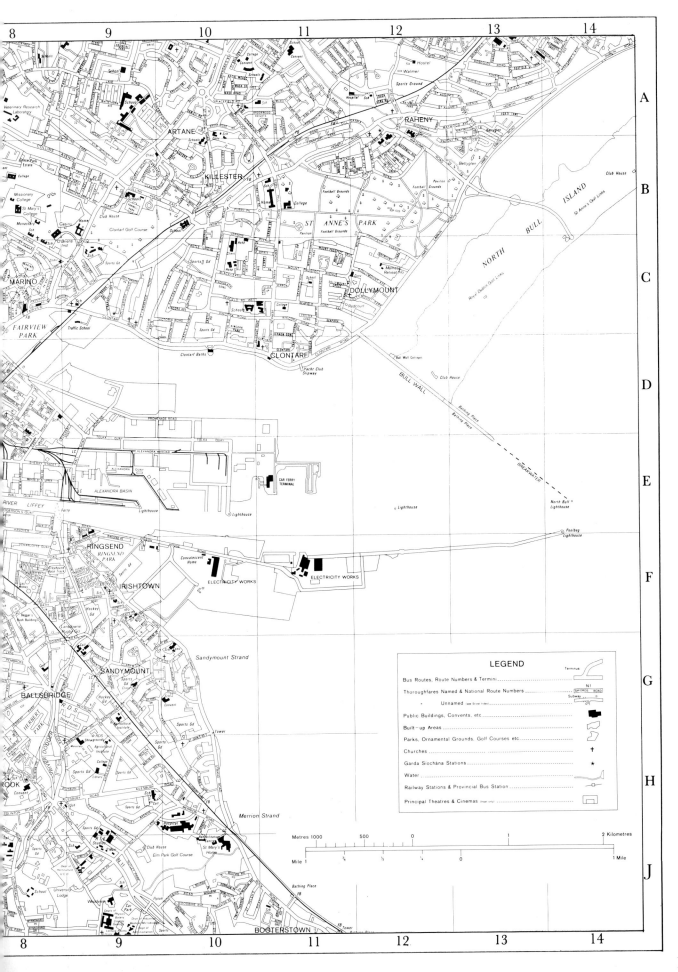

"Ah, but she was the queer old skeowsha anyhow, Anna Livia . . . and sure he was the quare old buntz too, Dear Dirty Dumpling . . . .".

(Finnegans Wake)